Informing the legislative debate since 1914 _____

The Obama Administration's Proposal to Establish a National Network for Manufacturing Innovation

John F. Sargent Jr.
Specialist in Science and Technology Policy

January 29, 2014

Congressional Research Service

7-5700

www.crs.gov

R42625

Summary

Manufacturing plays an important role in the nation's economy, employment, and national defense. Accordingly, Congress has maintained a strong interest in the health of the U.S. manufacturing sector. Some analysts have expressed concerns about a decades-long decline in manufacturing employment punctuated by a steep drop from 2001 to 2010, as well as about the offshore outsourcing of production and related functions, such as research and development, by U.S. manufacturers. Others see the U.S. manufacturing sector as vibrant and healthy as evidenced by growth in output and productivity.

The Obama Administration has undertaken a number of initiatives intended to support U.S. manufacturing, including establishment of the Advanced Manufacturing Partnership, Advanced Manufacturing National Program Office (AMNPO), Advanced Manufacturing Technology Consortia program, National Robotics Initiative, and Materials Genome Initiative.

In his FY2013 budget, President Obama proposed the creation of a National Network for Manufacturing Innovation (NNMI) to help accelerate innovation by investing in industrially relevant manufacturing technologies with broad applications, and to support manufacturing technology commercialization by bridging the gap between the laboratory and the market. Congress did not act on the President's proposal for FY2013. Nevertheless, the Administration used the Department of Defense's existing authorities and FY2012 regular appropriations to compete and award a pilot institute, the National Additive Manufacturing Innovation Institute, referring to it as "a proof-of-concept for the potential subsequent institutes."

In addition, the Administration sought nationwide input from key stakeholder groups to help guide the design of the NNMI. The AMNPO held four regional workshops and published a Request for Information (RFI) in the *Federal Register* inviting public comment on the proposed NNMI program. The input gathered from the workshops and the RFI was used by the AMNPO to prepare a National Science and Technology Committee report, *National Network for Manufacturing Innovation: A Preliminary Design*, published in January 2013.

In his 2014 budget request, President Obama again included the NNMI proposal. He also announced his intention to establish three additional manufacturing institutes in FY2013 using existing authorities and appropriations, two by the Department of Defense (DOD) and one by the Department of Energy (DOE). As in his FY2013 budget, the President's NNMI proposal calls for the establishment of up to 15 Institutes for Manufacturing Innovation (IMI) funded through a one-time infusion of $1 billion in mandatory funding to the Department of Commerce (DOC) National Institute for Standards and Technology (NIST) and to be spent over multiple years. Each IMI would be comprised of stakeholders from industry, academia, federal agencies, and state government entities. According to the proposal, each IMI is to be competitively selected, serve as a regional hub for manufacturing innovation (as well as part of the national network), and have a unique focus area (e.g., an advanced material, manufacturing process, enabling technology, or industry sector). Under the President's proposal, the NNMI would be managed collaboratively by NIST, DOD, DOE, the National Science Foundation, the National Aeronautics and Space Administration, and other agencies.

In August 2013, bills were introduced in the House (H.R. 2996) and Senate (S. 1468) to establish a Network for Manufacturing Innovation. The bills include identical provisions for establishing a Network for Manufacturing Innovation Program within the DOC's National Institute of Standards and Technology. Each bill was referred to committee(s); no further action had been taken on either bill at the time this report was published.

Contents

Tables

Contacts

Overview

Congress maintains a strong interest in the health of the U.S. manufacturing sector due to its central roles in the U.S. economy and national defense. Manufacturing accounts for about 12% of the nation's gross domestic product (GDP) and nearly two-thirds of U.S. exports. Manufacturing enterprises directly employ nearly 12 million U.S. workers and indirectly support millions of additional jobs in other industries (e.g., banking, shipping, insurance). Manufacturers also fund about two-thirds of the nation's industrial research and development (R&D), providing a foundation for technological innovation and continued U.S. technological leadership. In addition, manufacturing workers earn higher annual wages ($47,240 in 2012) than the overall annual wages for U.S. workers ($45,790).[1] Similarly, total compensation (wages and benefits) for manufacturing workers ($79,390) exceeds total compensation for all employees ($69,710).[2] With respect to national defense, the United States depends heavily on its manufacturing base to produce the weapons, aircraft, vehicles, ships, and other equipment needed to protect the nation.

Analysts hold divergent views of the health of U.S. manufacturing. Some see the U.S. manufacturing sector as vibrant and healthy. Those holding this view tend to point to, among other things, the sector's strong growth in output and productivity, as well as the United States' world-leading share of global manufacturing output.[3] In addition, between January 2010 and November 2013, manufacturing employment added approximately 554,000 jobs, growing to more than 12.0 million.[4]

Other analysts believe that the U.S. manufacturing sector is at risk. Expressed concerns of those holding this view include:

- a "hollowing-out" of U.S. manufacturing resulting from the decision of many U.S. manufacturers to move production activities offshore and other corporate functions (e.g., research and development, accounting, information technology, tax planning, legal research);[5]

- focused efforts by other nations to grow the size, diversity, and technological prowess of their manufacturing capabilities, and to attract manufacturing operations of U.S.-headquartered multinational companies using a variety of policy tools (e.g., tax holidays, worker training incentives, market access, access to rare earth minerals); and

- a decades-long declining trend in U.S. manufacturing employment, punctuated by a steeper drop from 2001 to 2010. In January 2010, U.S. manufacturing

---

[1] Occupational Employment Statistics, May 2012, Bureau of Labor Statistics, U.S. Department of Labor, http://www.bls.gov/oes.

[2] CRS analysis of data from Table 6.2D (Compensation of Employees by Industry) and Table 6.5D (Full-Time Equivalent Employees by Industry), National Income and Product Accounts, Bureau of Economic Analysis, U.S. Department of Commerce, http://www.bea.gov/iTable/iTable.cfm?ReqID=9&step=1#reqid=9&step=1&isuri=1.

[3] For more information, see CRS Report R41898, *Job Creation in the Manufacturing Revival*, by Marc Levinson.

[4] Bureau of Labor Statistics, U.S. Department of Labor, Current Employment Statistics survey database, data for manufacturing employment, all employees, seasonally-adjusted, http://data.bls.gov/cgi-bin/surveymost.

[5] For more information, see CRS Report R41712, *"Hollowing Out" in U.S. Manufacturing: Analysis and Issues for Congress*, by Marc Levinson.

employment fell to its lowest level (11.5 million) since March 1941, down more than 41% from its peak of 19.6 million in June 1979.[6]

The recent recession, relatively slow pace of recovery, and concerns about the prospects for double-dip recession[7] have contributed to increased concerns about the health of U.S. manufacturing. Some stakeholders and policy makers advocate for macro-level changes to improve the business environment, including reducing tax and regulatory burdens on manufacturers and reforming the nation's tort laws.

Others—including President Obama—support more direct and focused efforts funded by the federal government. In particular, President Obama has undertaken and proposed the creation and funding of a variety of initiatives (e.g., the Advanced Manufacturing Partnership, the National Robotics Initiative, Materials Genome Initiative) to help address concerns about U.S. manufacturing. One of the President's key proposals to help U.S. manufacturers is the establishment of a National Network for Manufacturing Innovation (NNMI).

In February 2012, the Obama Administration released *A National Strategic Plan for Advanced Manufacturing*, a report by the National Science and Technology Council (NSTC), putting forth a strategy to guide federal advanced manufacturing R&D investments. The report notes

> The acceleration of innovation for advanced manufacturing requires bridging a number of gaps in the present U.S. innovation system, particularly the gap between R&D activities and the deployment of technological innovations in domestic production of goods.[8]

The proposed NNMI seeks, in part, to bridge the innovation gap asserted in this report.

Some policy makers may oppose the NNMI for a variety of reasons, including concerns about the federal budget deficit; the appropriate role of the federal government; potential market distortions, inefficiency, and waste; and the subsidization of for-profit corporations and their shareholders at the expense of taxpayers. These issues are discussed later in this report. (See "Issues for Consideration.")

Administration Proposal

President Obama first proposed the establishment of a National Network for Manufacturing Innovation in his FY2013 budget, requesting $1 billion in mandatory funding[9] to support the establishment of up to 15 institutes. He formally introduced the concept on March 9, 2012, in a speech at the Rolls-Royce Crosspointe jet engine disc manufacturing facility in Virginia.

---

[6] See footnote 3.

[7] For additional information about the recession and the subsequent pace of economic growth, see CRS Report R41444, *Double-Dip Recession: Previous Experience and Current Prospect*, by Craig K. Elwell.

[8] NSTC, Executive Office of the President, *A National Strategic Plan for Advanced Manufacturing*, February 2012, p. 1, http://www.whitehouse.gov/sites/default/files/microsites/ostp/iam_advancedmanufacturing_strategicplan_2012.pdf.

[9] Mandatory spending is controlled by laws other than appropriations acts, often through authorizing legislation. Authorizing legislation establishes or continues the operation of a federal program or agency, either indefinitely or for a specified period. In contrast, discretionary spending is provided and controlled through the annual appropriations process. For additional information on mandatory funding, see CRS Report RL33074, *Mandatory Spending Since 1962*, by Mindy R. Levit and D. Andrew Austin.

Subsequently, the Department of Defense issued a solicitation and made an award in FY2012 for "A Pilot Institute for the National Network for Manufacturing Innovation" focused on additive manufacturing. (See "The National Additive Manufacturing Innovation Institute: A Pilot NNMI Institute" later in this report for a more detailed discussion.) In addition, in the absence of congressional action on his FY2013 proposal, President Obama announced that three additional institutes would be competed and awarded in 2013—two by the Department of Defense (DOD) and one by the Department of Energy (DOE)—using existing authorities and FY2013 appropriations. (See "Affiliated Centers to be Awarded in FY2014" later in this report for a more detailed discussion.)

In his FY2014 budget, President Obama once again proposed $1 billion in mandatory funding to support the establishment of the NNMI with up to 15 institutes. According to the President's proposal, the purpose of the NNMI is to bring together industry, universities and community colleges, federal agencies, and regional and state organizations

> to develop new manufacturing technologies with broad applications. Each institute will have a unique technology focus. These institutes will help support an ecosystem of manufacturing activity in local areas. The Manufacturing Innovation Institutes will support manufacturing technology commercialization by allowing new manufacturing processes and technologies to progress more smoothly from basic research to implementation in manufacturing.
>
> The NNMI Federal investment is designed to catalyze industry and non-federal co-investment in advanced manufacturing. Each institute is expected to have a plan to become self-sustaining and fully independent of NNMI Federal funds five to seven years after launch.[10]

In particular, the NNMI seeks to "advance technological innovation at a pace much faster than any one company could on its own,"[11] integrate innovation resources, improve the competitiveness of U.S. manufacturing, and encourage investment in the United States.[12] The NNMI is to be managed collaboratively by the Department of Commerce's (DOC's) National Institute of Standards and Technology (NIST), DOD, DOE, National Science Foundation (NSF), the National Aeronautics and Space Administration (NASA), and other agencies through the Advanced Manufacturing National Program Office (AMNPO),[13] a multi-agency coordination office.[14]

---

[10] *Budget of the United States Government, Fiscal Year 2014*, Appendix, p. 226, http://www.whitehouse.gov/sites/default/files/omb/budget/fy2014/assets/com.pdf.

[11] Testimony of Patrick D. Gallagher, Under Secretary for Standards and Technology, DOC, before the U.S. Congress, House Committee on Science, Space, and Technology, Subcommittee on Technology and Innovation, *Assembling the Facts: Examining the Proposed National Network for Manufacturing Innovation*, 112th Cong., 2nd sess., May 31, 2012.

[12] NIST, "Request for Information on Proposed New Program: National Network for Manufacturing Innovation (NNMI)," *Federal Register*, Vol. 77, No. 87, pp. 26509-26511, May 4, 2012, https://federalregister.gov/a/2012-10809.

[13] The AMNPO is a multi-agency coordination office hosted by the Department of Commerce National Institute of Standards and Technology (DOC/NIST). AMNPO participating agencies include DOC/NIST, Department of Defense (DOD), Department of Education (ED), Department of Energy (DOE), National Aeronautics and Space Administration (NASA), and the National Science Foundation (NSF).

[14] *From Discovery to Scale-up: About the National Network for Manufacturing Innovation*, Advanced Manufacturing Portal, http://www.manufacturing.gov/nnmi_overview.html.

Funding

As proposed in the President's FY2014 budget, NIST would receive a one-time infusion of $1 billion in mandatory funding in FY2014 to be spent over nine years (see **Table 1**). Federal funds would be used to help establish and support up to 15 Institutes for Manufacturing Innovation (IMIs, which collectively would form the NNMI) on a cost-shared basis with industrial, academic, and state and local organization partners. Each IMI is expected to become financially sustainable within seven years of its launch through income-generating activities such as member fees, intellectual property licenses, contract research, and fee-for-service activities.[15]

Table 1. Proposed Schedule of NNMI Expenditures

in millions of dollars

FY2014	FY2015	FY2016	FY2017	FY2018	FY2019	FY2020	FY2021	FY2022
38	112	180	186	156	122	102	74	30

Source: Office of Management and Budget, Executive Office of the President, *Fiscal Year 2014 Budget of the U.S. Government*, April 2013, Table S-9, p. 203.

Model

The NNMI is said by some to be modeled after the German Fraunhofer Institutes (see "The Fraunhofer-Gesellschaft Model" box below), which some consider to be a key facet of Germany's high-tech manufacturing success.[16] The Council on Competitiveness,[17] Information Technology and Innovation Foundation,[18] and President's Council of Advisors on Science and Technology[19] and other organizations have endorsed the NNMI concept or proposed a network of U.S.-based public-private manufacturing centers similar to the NNMI.

---

[15] *Budget of the United States Government, Fiscal Year 2014*, Appendix, p. 226, http://www.whitehouse.gov/sites/default/files/omb/budget/fy2014/assets/com.pdf; *National Network for Manufacturing Innovation: A Preliminary Design*, AMNPO, NSTC, Executive Office of the President, January 2013, p. ii, http://www.whitehouse.gov/sites/default/files/microsites/ostp/nstc_nnmi_prelim_design_final.pdf.

[16] U.S. Congress, House Committee on Science, Space, and Technology, Subcommittee on Technology and Innovation, *Assembling the Facts: Examining the Proposed National Network for Manufacturing Innovation*, 112th Cong., 2nd sess., May 31, 2012, http://democrats.science.house.gov/sites/democrats.science.house.gov/files/documents/NNMI%20Hearing%20Opening%20Statement-FINAL%20WEBSITE.pdf.

[17] Council on Competitiveness, *Make: An American Manufacturing Movement*, Washington, DC, December 2011, pp. 63-64, http://www.compete.org/images/uploads/File/PDF%20Files/USMCI_Make.pdf.

[18] The Information Technology and Innovation Foundation, *A Charter for Revitalizing American Manufacturing*, Washington, DC, 2011, p. 2; and "ITIF Welcomes President Obama's Proposal on Manufacturing Innovation," press release, March 9, 2012, http://www.itif.org/pressrelease/itif-welcomes-president-obamas-proposal-manufacturing-innovation.

[19] President's Council of Advisors on Science and Technology, *Report to the President on Ensuring American Leadership in Advanced Manufacturing*, Washington, DC, June 2011, http://www.whitehouse.gov/sites/default/files/microsites/ostp/pcast-advanced-manufacturing-june2011.pdf.

The Fraunhofer-Gesellshaft Model

The Fraunhofer-Gesellschaft* is a German-based, application-oriented research organization that seeks to bridge the innovation gap that can exist between fundamental research activities and commercial applications. In particular, Fraunhofer illustrates the position of its work along the innovation path as being between Germany's Max-Planck Institutes, which conduct fundamental basic research, and industry, and its sources of funding as being balanced between public and private sources. (See graphic below.)

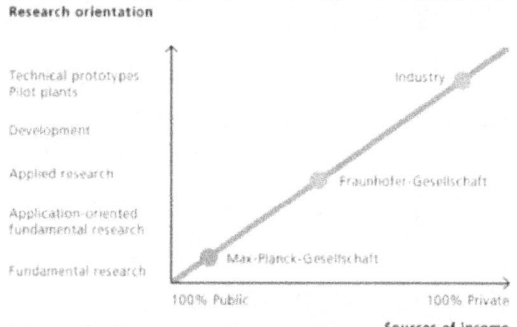

Fraunhofer has 66 institutes and research units with more than 22,000 staff members. Fraunhofer reports its annual research budget as €1.9 billion (approximately $2.5 billion). More than 70% of Fraunhofer's funding is provided through contract research with industry and publicly-financed research projects; the balance is provided by the German federal and Länder (state) governments as base funding used to support longer-term, pre-competitive research. According to Fraunhofer, the institutes bolster the competitive strength of the economy in their local regions, and throughout Germany and Europe, by promoting innovation, strengthening the technology base, improving the acceptance of new technologies, and helping to train scientists and engineers.

Fraunhofer has three subsidiaries, including Fraunhofer USA, a wholly owned non-profit organization headquartered in Plymouth, Michigan. As of 2011, Fraunhofer USA operated six centers in the United States, each working in collaboration with one or more Fraunhofer Institutes in Germany. Total 2011 revenues for Fraunhofer USA were €37.5 million (approximately $48.6 million), of which €16.1 million (approximately $20.9 million) were posted by the Fraunhofer Center for Molecular Biotechnology in Delaware, and €7.3 million (approximately $9.5 million) by the Fraunhofer Center for Sustainable Energy Systems in Massachusetts.

* "Gesellschaft" is a German word meaning association, society, or institute.

Sources: Fraunhofer-Gesellschaft website, http://www.fraunhofer.de; Fraunhofer *Annual Report 2011*.

Administration's *Preliminary Design* for the NNMI

In 2012, the Advanced Manufacturing National Program Office sought nationwide input from industry, academia, state and regional governments, economic development authorities, industry associations and consortia, private citizens, and other interested parties to help guide the design of the NNMI. The AMNPO held four regional workshops and published a Request for Information (RFI) in the *Federal Register* inviting public comment on the proposed NNMI program.[20] A total of 875 people attended the workshops and the RFI drew 78 responses representing the viewpoints of more than 100 separate entities.[21]

The input gathered from the workshops and the RFI was used by the AMNPO in the preparation of a National Science and Technology Committee report, *National Network for Manufacturing Innovation: A Preliminary Design,* hereinafter the *Preliminary Design* report, published in January 2013 that articulates the Administration's perspective of the principles and characteristics for the NNMI program.[22] According to the AMNPO, the document also "builds on a review of

---

[20] *Federal Register*, Vol. 77, No. 87, pp. 26509-26511, May 4, 2012, https://federalregister.gov/a/2012-10809.

[21] RFI Responses & Workshop Reports, Advanced Manufacturing Portal, http://manufacturing.gov/rfi_responses html.

[22] *National Network for Manufacturing Innovation: A Preliminary Design*, AMNPO, NSTC, EOP, January 2013.

---

best practices used to establish the pilot institute" (the National Additive Manufacturing Innovation Institute [NAMMI]); see "The National Additive Manufacturing Innovation Institute: A Pilot NNMI Institute" later in this report for further information.

The following sections provide an overview of selected concepts and characteristics presented in the NNMI *Preliminary Design* report.

Concepts

The *Preliminary Design* report articulates a number of broad concepts for the NNMI. According to the report, the National Network for Manufacturing Innovation is to be composed of competitively selected, independently managed Institutes for Manufacturing Innovation (IMIs or institutes). Each IMI would have a specific focus area (discussed in detail below) and serve as a regional innovation hub. Collectively the institutes are to function as a network for the sharing of knowledge and best practices. The size and scale of the NNMI is intended to provide long-term regional and national economic impact.

According to the National Science and Technology Council, "A gap exists between R&D activities and the deployment of technological innovations in domestic production of goods" that is detrimental to U.S. innovation, trade, and competitiveness.[23] According to the *Preliminary Design* report, the proposed NNMI seeks to bridge this gap by strengthening support for R&D that lies between the discovery and invention stages of innovation and the manufacturing innovation and scale up stages that precede commercialization.

The *Preliminary Design* report states that the IMIs (or institutes) are to be long-term partnerships between industry and academia (including universities and community colleges) enabled by federal, state, and local governments. The network and individual IMIs are to have a strong focus on building clusters of advanced manufacturing capabilities that join expertise from industry, academia, and government. The NNMI's emphasis is to be on linking and integrating existing public and private resources into a robust national innovation ecosystem. The IMIs are to serve as regional nodes of advanced manufacturing capabilities, where the processes to build next-generation products will be developed, demonstrated, and refined to the point where there is a clearer, lower-risk path to commercial-scale manufacturing. IMIs are to leverage existing regional or national innovation systems or catalyze the formation and sustainability of new innovation clusters. IMIs are to offer facilities comprising an "industrial commons" (the R&D, engineering, and manufacturing capabilities needed to turn inventions into competitive, manufacturable commercial products) to accelerate the formation and growth of small- and medium-sized enterprises (SMEs), and are to integrate education and workforce training functions into their operations.

---

[23] NSTC, Executive Office of the President, *A National Strategic Plan for Advanced Manufacturing*, February 2012, p. 1, http://www.whitehouse.gov/sites/default/files/microsites/ostp/iam_advancedmanufacturing_strategicplan_2012.pdf.

Among the other concepts put forward in the *Preliminary Design* report:

- IMIs are to be based upon concepts of open innovation and partnership.

- IMIs are to facilitate the formation of effective teams of industrial and academic experts from multiple disciplines to solve difficult problems, from pre-competitive industrially relevant research to proprietary technology development for product manufacturing.

- IMIs are to provide shared-use facilities with the goal of scaling up laboratory demonstrations and maturing technologies for manufacture.

- IMIs are to create, showcase, and deploy new capabilities, new products, and new processes that can impact commercial production.

- IMIs are to engage and assist small and medium-sized enterprises in applying and adapting new manufacturing process technologies by providing technical assistance, trained personnel, and access to shared equipment and infrastructure.

- Through dual appointment of faculty and students in both research universities and IMIs, the IMIs are to develop leaders familiar with research applications, new technologies, and production systems.

- Each IMI is to have a specific physical location or locations and a clear lead organization, rather than existing as a "virtual" or distributed organization. At the same time, IMIs are to collaborate with organizations in any location that have relevant, complementary expertise.

Focus Areas

With respect to focus areas, the NNMI *Preliminary Design* report states that each IMI is to have a unique and well-defined focus area, such as a manufacturing process (e.g., additive manufacturing), an enabling technology (e.g., nanotechnology), manufacturing processes for new advanced materials (e.g., carbon nanotubes), or an industry sector (e.g., medical devices). IMI focus areas are to be defined by the proposing teams, driven by the needs of industry, the opportunities created by new technologies, and the programmatic needs of the AMNPO partners.

Selection Process

With respect to the process of selecting IMIs, the NNMI *Preliminary Design* report states that Institutes are to be chosen through an open, competitive application process. The solicitation and evaluation process is to be managed by the AMNPO partner agencies. Proposals are to be evaluated competitively by a review team that includes members of the AMNPO, agency partners, and other experts. The merit-based selection process may include pre-proposals, site visits, and economic and business plan analyses.

According to the *Preliminary Design* report, evaluation criteria for IMI proposals are expected to include the proposed focus area and its importance to the American economy; the plan for significant production-scale manufacturing impact in its area of specialization with respect to research, commercialization, and workforce training; the effectiveness of the governance and management structures; the proposed resources; the level of co-investment; engagement with

SMEs and other community stakeholders; and the strength of the plan with respect to achieving sustainability.

IMI Leads and Stakeholders

According to the *Preliminary Design* report, IMIs are to be led by an independent, U.S. not-for-profit institution with the capacity to lead an industry-wide technology, workforce development, and infrastructure agenda. Partners in the IMI are to include manufacturing enterprises of all sizes, including startups; a diverse set of institutions of higher education including both research universities and community colleges; research organizations (including federally funded research and development centers, subject to statutory or regulatory restrictions); national laboratories or government agencies (subject to funding restrictions); career and technical institutions; state, regional, and local public and private entities that support industrial clusters and associated economic development partnerships; unions; professional and industry associations; other not-for-profit organizations; and the general public. To help ensure a broad impact, IMIs are to openly encourage the addition of new partners and participants wherever relevant through well-defined mechanisms.

In addition, the report states that IMIs are envisioned as hubs linking the national and international resources that exist within the area of focus of the institute. IMIs are to leverage industry consortia, regional clusters, and other resources in science, technology, and economic development. In particular, IMIs should seek to benefit and leverage the various centers and research institutions funded through existing federal programs, such as the National Science Foundation's Engineering Research Centers (ERC) and Industry/University Cooperative Research Centers (I/UCRC) programs.

With respect to stakeholder participation, the *Preliminary Design* report states that IMIs are to demonstrate meaningful outreach to and engagement with SMEs. Each IMI is expected to engage existing intermediaries, centers, and networks that work with and address the needs of SMEs, such as the NIST Hollings Manufacturing Extension Partnership network and state and regional technology-based economic development programs. Institutes also are to be encouraged, to the extent appropriate, to seek out successful SBIR awardees to support their alignment with supply chains and explore opportunities for evolutionary demonstration of SBIR technologies within an institute's focus area.

The *Preliminary Design* report envisions IMIs assisting SMEs in a variety of ways, including, for example, information about technology trends; access to cutting edge technologies that assist with process innovations and development; shared facilities and access to specialized equipment that can accelerate product design, prototyping, and testing; and technical advice and assistance. The report also states that SMEs interested in a broad range of services and an ongoing relationship might participate in an IMI tiered membership structure that would minimize barriers to entry and encourage the membership of SMEs in the institute.

Foreign Participation

The NNMI *Preliminary Design* report states that participation in an institute by a non-domestic organization is to be allowed only when in the economic interest of the United States, as demonstrated by that organization's investments in the United States in research, development, and manufacturing; significant contributions to employment in the United States; and commitment that any technology arising from or assisted by the institute be used to promote domestic manufacturing activities. Participation restrictions for non-domestic organizations may exist in some circumstances.

Funding

With respect to funding, the NNMI *Preliminary Design* report notes that the President's proposal calls for a $1 billion investment from FY2014 to FY2022 to support up to 15 IMIs. Institutes are to be supported with cost-share funding from federal and non-federal sources. Each IMI is to be of sufficient size and scope to have major national and regional economic impacts and to address the multidimensional challenges associated with the institute's focus area. The level of federal funding will depend upon the magnitude of the opportunity, maturity, and capital intensity of the technology, and scope of the focus area of the institute. The report states that it expects institutes will typically receive a total of $70 million-$120 million in federal NNMI funds over five to seven years. When combined with the non-federal co-investment, the total capitalization of an IMI is expected to be in the range of $140 million to $240 million, based on a 1:1 matching of federal funding. The report states that it is likely that cooperative agreements will be the primary funding mechanism for awarding IMIs, although other types of grants and contracts may also be used.

According to the *Preliminary Design* report, each institute is to demonstrate significant co-investment support from non-federal sources during the period the institute receives federal funding. The non-federal co-investment—in cash and in-kind contributions—is to be tangible, meaningful, and in the aggregate, substantial enough to signal strong and committed industry, regional, and local partnership. In-kind and cash contributions may arise from any source, but are only counted as co-investment if they come from non-federal sources and directly support the function of the institute. The funds are to come from the IMI (e.g., revenues generated from the licensing of intellectual property); the members of the institute; state, regional, and local sources (such as economic development agencies); private donations; or other non-federal sources.

The report states that federal funding is expected to be initially larger when an institute is established and to diminish after the initial two to three years so that most of the institute's funds are provided by private and other funding sources as time progresses. Non-federal support is anticipated to be large at the time of award and primarily comprised of in-kind items such as equipment and buildings. Continuing federal funding under the NNMI program will be contingent on co-investment by businesses and other non-federal entities in an IMI, as well as the IMI's progress toward sustainable operations. Institutes are expected to be fully independent of federal NNMI funds and sustainable within seven years of launch through income-generating activities such as membership fees, intellectual property licenses, contract research, and fee-for-service activities. To encourage the transition to sustainability, the report states that a portion of the federal funds used for IMI projects is to be awarded competitively among the institutes. Competitive project award decisions are to be made in part based on the technical quality of proposals, as well as on prior institute performance and the strength of industrial participation.

Operation of the Network

With respect to the operation of the national network of IMIs, the NNMI *Preliminary Design* states that each IMI is to communicate best practices and coordinate efforts with other institutes; coordinate approaches on issues such as intellectual property treatment, contract research, and performance metrics; be led by independent, not-for-profit institutions that coordinate industry partners both locally and nationwide, including SMEs; focus upon workforce development with its industry and academic partners at the university and community college levels to impact the engineering and technical workforce; and join in the governance and activities of an NNMI-wide Network Leadership Council.

The report states that leadership from the institutes is to formally collaborate through a Network Leadership Council made up of representatives from the IMIs, federal agencies, and other entities as appropriate. The Network Leadership Council is to oversee efforts to develop consistent and common approaches for matters such as intellectual property, contracts, research and performance metrics, and facilitating the sharing of best practices.

In addition, the *Preliminary Design* report states that:

- Each IMI's research and commercialization outcomes are to be available to other IMIs as appropriate, through technology and knowledge transfer efforts.

- To the extent possible, the institutes are to work collaboratively, sharing resources, best practices, and research and development results. In particular, IMIs are to transparently share funding and membership models, annual reports, and projections.

- Each IMI is to participate in the AMNPO-hosted Manufacturing Portal, a web-based resource to help manufacturers locate relevant research, research partners, and pertinent information within the network.

Activities and Operations

With respect to the activities and operations of the NNMI, the *Preliminary Design* report states that each IMI is to focus on component validation in a relevant environment, system model or prototype demonstration in a relevant environment, system prototype demonstration in an operational environment, and actual system completion and qualification through test and demonstration.[24]

According to the report, IMI activities may include, but are not limited to:

- applied research, development, and demonstration projects that reduce the cost and risk of developing and implementing new technologies in advanced manufacturing;

- assessing the skills and certifications needed and providing educational opportunities to improve and expand the manufacturing workforce, including K-12 programs, internship opportunities, skills certification, community college engagement, university collaboration, graduate students, post-

---

[24] The activities of the institutes correspond to Technology Readiness Levels 4-7 and Manufacturing Readiness Levels 4-7, as defined in Department of Defense publications, *Technology Readiness Assessment (TRA) Deskbook* and *Manufacturing Readiness Level (MRL) Deskbook*. For additional information, see *Technology Readiness Assessment (TRA) Deskbook*, Office of the Director, Defense Research and Engineering, DOD, July 2009, http://www.skatelescope.org/public/2011-11-18_WBS-SOW_Development_Reference_Documents/ DoD_TRA_July_2009_Read_Version.pdf, and *Manufacturing Readiness Level (MRL) Deskbook, Version 2.0,* Manufacturing Technology Program, Office of the Secretary of Defense, DOD, May 2011, http://www.dodmrl.com/ MRL_Deskbook_V2.pdf.

doctoral students, and retraining to meet the requirements set forth by an institute's mission in order to impact both the technical and degreed engineering workforce;

- developing innovative methodologies and practices for increasing the capabilities and capacity of supply chain expansion and integration;

- providing access to shared facility infrastructure to help reduce the cost and risk of commercializing new technologies and to address relevant manufacturing challenges on a production-level scale; and

- facilitating the creation of start-up companies to commercialize R&D results.

Governance

With respect to governance of the IMIs, the *Preliminary Design* report states that the interests of the three broad stakeholders of NNMI—industry, academia, and government—need to be preserved through a joint governance model. IMIs are to have substantial autonomy from its partner organizations and institutions, including an independent fiduciary board of directors predominantly composed of industry representatives and a leader in charge of day-to-day operations. IMI proposals are to outline the methods by which institute decisions will be made, including those related to operations, membership, intellectual property, capital investments, project selection, funding allocation, and sustainability.

According to the report, efficient operation of the NNMI network is to be facilitated through common policies. Common policies will facilitate interaction with SMEs, promote collaboration and movement within the network, and allow institutes to share services. While recognizing the differing needs of various manufacturing sectors, clusters, and ecosystems, the network will strive, as far as is practical, to maintain common policies with regard to intellectual property, contract research, operations, accountability, and marketing and branding.

Preliminary Activities

The Obama Administration has undertaken efforts to lay a foundation for the NNMI in advance of possible congressional authorization and funding. In addition to the outreach effort undertaken to provide stakeholders an opportunity to help shape the design of the NNMI (see "Administration's Preliminary Design for the NNMI"), the Administration proceeded in FY2012 with the establishment of a pilot institute, the National Additive Manufacturing Innovation Institute (NAMII). Subsequently, in his February 2013 State of the Union Address, President Obama announced his intention to create three additional manufacturing innovation institutes in FY2013. The new institutes are to be established using existing FY2013 appropriations and the general authorities of the two sponsoring agencies, DOD and DOE.[25] The NAMII and the plan for establishing the new manufacturing institutes are discussed below.

---

[25] In the absence of congressional authorization of the NNMI, the AMNPO is not referring to NAMII or the new centers as being IMIs within the NNMI, but rather as manufacturing institutes. The AMNPO asserts that the centers would be considered part of the NNMI, if the NNMI is authorized by Congress. Personal conversation between CRS and the AMNPO, May 2, 2013.

The National Additive Manufacturing Innovation Institute: A Pilot NNMI Institute

In his announcement of the NNMI in March 2012, President Obama also committed to the establishment of a pilot institute using existing resources from the Department of Defense and other federal agencies.[26] In May 2012, DOD published a broad agency announcement (BAA, a tool used for contracting) soliciting technical and cost proposals for an Additive Manufacturing Innovation Institute, describing it as "the first institute to be launched within the National Network for Manufacturing Innovation" and "a proof-of-concept for the potential subsequent institutes."[27] (The BAA described additive manufacturing as "a revolutionary suite of manufacturing technologies for building up parts, and potentially entire systems, in a layer-by-layer fashion, placing material precisely as directed by a 3D digital file.") Additive manufacturing is also sometimes referred to as "3-D printing."

On August 16, 2012, the White House announced the winning proposal, the National Additive Manufacturing Innovation Institute (NAMII), a partnership led by the National Center for Defense Manufacturing and Machining (NCDMM), based in Youngstown, OH. NAMII partners include 40 companies, 9 research universities, 5 community colleges, and 11 non-profit organizations. NAMII partners are located primarily in the Western Pennsylvania, Northeast Ohio, and Northern West Virginia region. Under the award, NAMII will receive $30 million in initial federal funding.[28] According to NDCMM, NAMII is committed to providing an additional $39 million as a cost share with funds provide mostly by industry and the states of Ohio, Pennsylvania, and West Virginia. In addition, once the institute is established it would be a "likely candidate for additional funds on a competitive basis"—up to $15 million in federal funding for specific projects.[29] These additional funds bring total potential federal funding to $45 million.

The lead agency for this institute is the Office of the Secretary of Defense (OSD), Manufacturing and Industrial Base Policy, through OSD Manufacturing Technology. The pilot institute administration is to be a cross-agency effort, primarily led by the Defense-wide Manufacturing Science and Technology Program Office, executed through the Air Force Research Laboratory. Other agencies providing funding and partnering with DOD to support NAMII include DOE, NASA, NSF, and NIST.

Affiliated Centers to be Awarded in FY2014

In February 2012, President Obama announced his intention to award three new manufacturing institutes using existing FY2013 funds and statutory authorities. On May 9, 2013, the White

---

[26] President Barack Obama, *Remarks by the President on Manufacturing and the Economy*, The White House, Petersburg, VA, March 9, 2012, http://www.whitehouse.gov/the-press-office/2012/03/09/remarks-president-manufacturing-and-economy.

[27] *A Pilot Institute for the National Network for Manufacturing Innovation (NNMI)*, Solicitation Number BAA-12-17-PKM, Department of the Air Force, Air Force Materiel Command, May 8, 2012, https://www.fbo.gov/?s=opportunity&mode=form&id=2bbada5cae4ab97438dc3f57fed050d0.

[28] The BAA restricts the use of federal funding to direct support of the goals of the institute, for applied research, education and training, and infrastructure development, and explicitly prohibits the use of government funds to build buildings or to buy land or facilities.

[29] Testimony of Patrick D. Gallagher, Under Secretary for Standards and Technology, DOC, before the U.S. Congress, May 31, 2012.

House announced competitions for two DOD manufacturing institutes—one focused on Digital Manufacturing and Design Innovation (DMDI) and the other focused on Lightweight and Modern Metals Manufacturing Innovation (LM3I)—and one DOE manufacturing institute focused on Next Generation Power Electronics Manufacturing.[30]

DOD Digital Manufacturing and Design Innovation Institute

According to DOD, the DMDI Institute is expected to focus on "enterprise-wide utilization of the digital thread, enabling highly integrated manufacturing and design of complex products at reduced cost and time."[31] The core technology areas of interest include, but are not limited to, advanced manufacturing enterprise, intelligent machines, advanced analysis, and cyber-physical security. The DMDI Institute is sponsored by the Office of the Secretary of Defense and led by the Department of the Army.

The Department of the Army issued a Request for Information (RFI) for the DMDI Institute on May 9, 2013.[32] On July 5, the Army issued a Broad Agency Announcement (BAA) (BAA Announcement Number BAA-13-01DMDI) soliciting proposals for the DMDI.

DOD Lightweight and Modern Metals Manufacturing Innovation Institute

The LM3I Institute is expected to focus on the integrated design and manufacturing of lightweight components and structures for commercial and defense applications, and the verification of those designs through pilot production and validation through experimental testing. The key areas of interest for the LM3I Institute are rapidly maturing and demonstrating production scale-up of existing, innovative, lightweight alloys; shortening the time necessary to design, integrate, and evaluate novel, affordable metals; developing more affordable, competitive automated manufacturing processes relevant to lightweight and modern metals; and developing the tools, skills, and knowledge base within the materials design and manufacturing workforce to use an integrated computational materials engineering infrastructure efficiently and effectively. The LM3I Institute is sponsored by the Office of Naval Research (ONR), in collaboration with the Office of the Secretary of Defense, Deputy Assistant Secretary of Defense, Manufacturing, and Industrial Base Policy.

The ONR issued an RFI for the LM3I Institute on May 9, 2013.[33] On July 2, 2013, the ONR issued a BAA (BAA Announcement Number ONRBAA13-019) soliciting proposals for the LM3I.

---

[30] Office of the Press Secretary, The White House, "Obama Administration Launches Competition for Three New Manufacturing Innovation Institutes," press release, May 9, 2013, http://www.whitehouse.gov/the-press-office/2013/05/09/obama-administration-launches-competition-three-new-manufacturing-innova.

[31] The "digital thread" refers to digital information about a manufactured good that flows with it through conceptual design, detail design, manufacturing, maintenance, repair, and operation.

[32] Army Contracting Command, Department of the Army, "Request for Information (RFI) Digital Manufacturing and Design Innovation (Proposed Institute)," May 9, 2013, https://www.fbo.gov/?s=opportunity&mode=form&id=05872b72e4a220382fb6de25e1789db6&tab=core&_cview=0.

[33] Office of Naval Research, Department of the Navy, "Request for Information (RFI), 13-RFI-0001, Lightweight and Modern Metals Manufacturing Innovation (LM3I) Proposed Institute," May, 9, 2013, https://www.fbo.gov/?s=opportunity&mode=form&id=fa26efa577c37ce57238aeb15bf9043a&tab=core&_cview=0.

DOE Next Generation Power Electronics Manufacturing Institute

In January 2014, the Department of Energy awarded the Next Generation Power Electronics Manufacturing Institute to a consortium of businesses and universities, led by North Carolina State University. The Next Generation Power Electronics Manufacturing Institute is being supported by the DOE Advanced Manufacturing Office[34] as a part of the department's Clean Energy Manufacturing Initiative (CEMI). The language incorporated in the DOE Funding Opportunity Announcement contained extensive language linking it to the NNMI.

The institute will focus on circuit design, packaging, module manufacturing capabilities, and wafer test metrology equipment for wide bandgap semiconductor power electronics device fabrication and manufacturing. DOE anticipates providing $14 million in initial funding, and an additional $14 million in each of the following four years for a total of $70 million.[35]

In addition to President Obama's request for $1 billion in mandatory funding for NIST in FY2014 to support the establishment of up to 15 institutes under the NNMI program, the President proposed $192.5 million in FY2014 funding for the establishment of new CEMI Institutes. The explanatory statement for Division D (Energy and Water Development and Related Agencies) of the Consolidated Appropriations Act, 2014 (P.L. 113-76) directs the Department of Energy to support the "Innovative Manufacturing Initiative to the extent possible with available funds" and "encourages research that supports development of wide bandgap semiconductor technologies."[36]

Legislative Status

The creation of the NNMI depends on congressional authorization and funding. No action was taken by the 112th Congress on President Obama's FY2013 request to establish and fund the NNMI. The President renewed his call for an NNMI in his FY2014 budget, again seeking $1 billion in mandatory funding. The use of mandatory funding for the NNMI would allow funding to be provided by a law other than an appropriations bill, removing the funding decision from the regular appropriations process.[37]

In August 2013, bills were introduced in the House (H.R. 2996) and Senate (S. 1468) to establish a Network for Manufacturing Innovation. Each bill would establish a Network for Manufacturing Innovation Program within the DOC's National Institute of Standards and Technology. As introduced, each bill contains identical provisions for the establishment of the program.

The bills identify a variety of purposes to be served by the program, including:

---

[34] The AMO is a part of the DOE Office of Energy Efficiency and Renewable Energy (EERE).

[35] Advanced Manufacturing Office, Office of Energy Efficiency and Renewable Energy, DOE, "Funding Opportunity Announcement—Clean Energy Manufacturing Initiative," DE-FOA-0000683, CFDA Number 81.086, May 9, 2013.

[36] Explanatory statement for Division D of P.L. 113-76, http://docs.house.gov/billsthisweek/20140113/113-HR3547-JSOM-D-F.pdf.

[37] Mandatory spending is controlled by laws other than appropriations acts, often through authorizing legislation. Authorizing legislation establishes or continues the operation of a federal program or agency, either indefinitely or for a specified period. In contrast, discretionary spending is provided and controlled through the annual appropriations process. For additional information on mandatory funding, see CRS Report RL33074, *Mandatory Spending Since 1962*, by Mindy R. Levit and D. Andrew Austin.

- improving the competitiveness of United States manufacturing and increasing domestic production;

- stimulating United States leadership in advanced manufacturing research, innovation, and technology;

- facilitating the transition of innovative technologies into scalable, cost-effective, and high-performing manufacturing capabilities;

- facilitating access by manufacturing enterprises to capital-intensive infrastructure, including high-performance computing, in order to improve the speed with which such enterprises commercialize new processes and technologies;

- accelerating the development of an advanced manufacturing workforce;

- facilitating peer exchange of and the documentation of best practices in addressing advanced manufacturing challenges; and

- leveraging non-federal sources of support to promote a stable and sustainable business model without the need for long-term federal funding.

The bills would direct the Secretary of Commerce to establish a network of centers for manufacturing innovation to engage in:

- research, development, and demonstration projects, including proof-of-concept development and prototyping, to reduce the cost, time, and risk of commercializing new technologies and improvements in existing technologies, processes, products, and research and development of materials to solve pre-competitive industrial problems with economic or national security implications;

- development and implementation of education and training courses, materials, and programs;

- development of innovative methodologies and practices for supply chain integration and introduction of new technologies into supply chains;

- outreach to and engagement with small- and medium-sized manufacturing enterprises, in addition to large manufacturing enterprises; and

- other such other activities as the Secretary of Commerce, in consultation with federal departments and agencies whose missions contribute to or are affected by advanced manufacturing, considers consistent with the program's purposes.

Other provisions of the bills include:

- authorize the participation of representatives from industrial entities, research universities, community colleges, and such other entities as the Secretary considers appropriate, which may include career and technical education schools, federal laboratories, state, local, and tribal governments, businesses, educational institutions, and nonprofit organizations;

- authorize the Secretary of Commerce to award financial assistance to assist in planning, establishing, or supporting a center for manufacturing innovation;

- require the use of a competitive, merit review process in the selection of centers;

- limit financial assistance under the program to no more than seven years;

- establish a National Office of the Network for Manufacturing Innovation Program, led by a Director, to oversee and carry out the program;

- require each center receiving financial assistance from the program to report annually to the Secretary of Commerce on its expenditures and performance with respect to its goals, plans, financial support, and accomplishments, as well as to how the center has furthered the authorized purposes of the program;

- require the Secretary of Commerce to prepare an annual report to Congress on the performance of the program;

- require the Government Accountability Office to perform a triennial assessment of the program reporting on the management, coordination, and industry utility of the program; assessing the extent to which the program has furthered its authorized purposes; and recommending legislative and administrative actions to improve the program;

- authorize the establishment of a Network for Manufacturing Innovation Fund and authorize appropriations of $600 million for the execution of the program; and

- designate the National Additive Manufacturing Innovation Institute and manufacturing centers currently under interagency review as centers for manufacturing innovation.

Following the introduction S. 1468, the bill was referred to the Senate Committee on Commerce, Science, and Transportation. Similarly, following its introduction, H.R. 2996 was referred to the House Committee on Science, Space, and Technology's Subcommittee on Research and Technology and the House Committee on Appropriations. No further action had been taken on either bill at the time this report was published.

On July 18, 2013, the Senate Committee on Appropriations reported S. 1329, the FY2014 appropriations act for the Department of Commerce, Department of Justice, and Science and Related Agencies. In the report accompanying the bill (S.Rept. 113-78), the committee asserts that there is "no significant distinction" between the proposed NNMI institutes and the Administration's Advanced Manufacturing Technology (AMTech) consortia. The report directs NIST to report within 60 days of enactment of the legislation "on how NNMI-related efforts can be merged into AmTech."[38]

Issues for Consideration

The proposed National Network for Manufacturing Innovation raises a variety of issues for Congress, some of which were raised in a hearing on the proposal held by the House Committee on Science, Space, and Technology's Subcommittee on Technology and Innovation in May 2012. Among the questions Congress may wish to consider if it takes up legislation to establish and fund the NNMI:

---

[38] S.Rept. 113-78.

- **What is the U.S. global competitive position in manufacturing?**

  Some assert that U.S. manufacturing is healthy and growing, pointing to indicators such as increased output and productivity; others assert that U.S. manufacturing is in decline, pointing to decreased manufacturing employment and the movement of production and related functions to other countries.

  Those who see U.S. manufacturing as healthy generally assert that increased globalization and efforts to facilitate trade naturally lead companies seeking to maximize profits, open new markets, increase global market share, and better serve their customers to locate some of their production and related activities outside the United States. They also argue that, in competing against other multinational corporations, they must undertake such efforts to remain competitive. Some also argue that a variety of factors in the U.S. market (e.g., tax rates, regulations, tort law) place a heavy burden on U.S. manufacturing; in contrast, other nations may have much lower labor costs and their governments may offer a variety of incentives (e.g., tax holidays, worker training, rapid permitting) to attract and retain the manufacturing and related activities of U.S.-based companies.

  Many who see U.S. manufacturing in decline assert that U.S. manufacturing capacity is being "hollowed out" as production facilities and supporting functions (such as R&D, information technology, and accounting) are sited overseas, leaving only a shell of a corporation located physically in the United States. Some experts assert that a nation's (or a state's or a region's) manufacturing strength depends on a "critical mass" of companies that are engaged in similar and supporting activities. This critical mass creates a synergy that increases the overall strength of the firms in the cluster due to a number of positive reinforcing factors (e.g., knowledge sharing, attraction of workforce talent, new start-ups, establishment of new plants, co-location of supply chains, improvements in infrastructure). As U.S.-based firms move production and related activities outside the United States, some believe that this "critical mass" may be lost, starting a downward spiral in which the synergies are lost and firms opt to move operations outside the United States where such clusters have developed.

  Accordingly, many who subscribe to this view believe that manufacturing employment will decline, R&D activities will relocate to be near production facilities, and service firms that support manufacturing will be lost. In addition, some assert that the "hollowing out" will result in the loss of manufacturing capabilities needed to support the nation's military and increase the manufacturing know-how of potential adversaries.

- **Should the federal government directly or indirectly support the competitive position of the U.S. manufacturing sector? Which federal policies and programs should be prioritized? Why should the NNMI be prioritized over other approaches? Is the NNMI duplicative of other federal efforts?**

  There are many views as to what the federal government can and should do to support the competitive position of the U.S. manufacturing sector. In general, some prefer an approach that reduces costs and other burdens on manufacturers, such as reducing taxes, regulations, and frivolous lawsuits. Others prefer an expanded direct role for the federal government. This could include increasing federal funding for manufacturing R&D, providing grants and loan guarantees for domestic manufacturing, and, in some cases, subsidizing production of products for which there are deemed positive benefits for the nation that cannot be captured by the manufacturer (economists refer to such benefits as positive externalities). With a range of options that might be pursued to improve the competitive position and strength of U.S.

manufacturing, some contend that the NNMI should be given high priority due to its perceived benefits (e.g., advancing research discoveries toward market-ready technologies).

Others may believe that the NNMI is not the right approach to bolstering U.S. manufacturing. Some may assert that the role envisioned for the NNMI should be performed by the private sector; that the federal government should not favor or subsidize particular companies, industries, or technologies; that the NNMI would be ineffective or counterproductive; that the funds that would go to the NNMI should be used to support manufacturing in other ways; that the funds should be used for different federal functions altogether; or that the funds should be directed toward deficit reduction. Some may believe that the NNMI is, in part or in whole, duplicative of other federal programs, such as the Manufacturing Extension Partnership; or, as a new and separate program, represents an increasing fragmentation of federal efforts to help manufacturers. Some may question whether additional federal funding will produce more innovation and whether and how the U.S. manufacturing base will effectively absorb such innovations.

The *Preliminary Design* report asserts that there are "notable distinctions" between the NNMI and federal manufacturing-related programs such as the NSF's Industry & University Cooperative Research (I/UCRC) and Engineering Research Centers (ERC), NIST Manufacturing Extension Partnership program, and other federal investments focused on basic and applied early stage research. Among the characteristics of the NNMI identified in the report that set it apart from other federal efforts: the scale of investment in each center, the specific focus on manufacturability and manufacturing processes and technologies; reliance on industry leadership, in partnership with other stakeholders; the significant industry co-investment which will "force [institutes] to have a pragmatic focus on industrially relevant technologies"; and the NNMI's education and workforce training approach that seeks to make community colleges an integral part of the effort. Congress may wish to explore the likely importance and effectiveness of these differentiating characteristics.

- **While the *Preliminary Design* report provides a broad outline of the functions that the network would serve and some of the roles of the federal government in the national network, other questions remain. For example: What authorities would the AMNPO have, if any, in the operation of the network? How would the federal government's role in NNMI network activity be funded? After the federal government's one-time funding is exhausted, what role would the federal government play in the network and how would this role be funded?**

Implicit in the title of the National Network for Manufacturing Innovation is the concept of a national network. The Administration's FY2013 proposal did not discuss how the individual institutes would function as a network. The January 2014 *Preliminary Design* report[39] provided some information about some of the functions of the network and the roles of the federal government. However, it did not specifically address funding source(s) for network activities or the types of authority that the AMNPO might have in executing these roles. Congress may want to explore what form the network would take (e.g., a national network office with staff, a database of information), what functions it would perform (e.g., sharing of lessons learned, referrals of companies to centers with specific expertise), which agencies/offices would perform each of the functions (e.g., NIST, AMNPO, IMIs), and how

---

[39] NSTC, Executive Office of the President, *A National Strategic Plan for Advanced Manufacturing*, February 2012, p. 1, http://www.whitehouse.gov/sites/default/files/microsites/ostp/iam_advancedmanufacturing_strategicplan_2012.pdf.

the performance of these functions would be paid for (e.g., the NNMI mandatory appropriation, agency general appropriations, private funding from the IMIs). In addition, Congress may opt to explore the role of the institutes in the operation of the national network.

- **Should the NNMI be funded on a mandatory or discretionary funding basis? Should a one-time advance appropriation be provided for the proposed life of the program, as proposed by President Obama, or should the NNMI be subject to annual review, oversight, and consideration in the regular annual appropriations process? Which programs would be cut or eliminated as offsets for the NNMI's proposed $1 billion mandatory appropriation?**

The NNMI could be supported through either mandatory[40] or discretionary funding. The Obama Administration has proposed one-time mandatory funding of $1 billion to be used over the course of nine years. This approach may provide a higher degree of certainty about the availability of out-year funding for the NNMI (though Congress could opt later to rescind all or part of such funding). Such an approach would require offsets from other mandatory funding. Alternatively, providing funding through annual appropriations might allow Congress greater oversight opportunities and flexibility in modifying the program and its funding levels. If the NNMI were to be supported through discretionary funding, cuts would need to be made from other discretionary spending. The Obama Administration's budget request specified a number of cuts in mandatory spending, but did not specify which cuts would be used to offset proposed funding for the NNMI.

- **What is the appropriate role of the federal government in manufacturing-related innovation? Should the federal government's role end with basic research funding, or include funding for applied research, development efforts focused on cost reduction and technical feasibility, or demonstration projects?**

There are many views regarding the appropriate role of the federal government in the innovation process. While there has been a general consensus on the federal government's support for basic research, congressional efforts to provide later-stage support for innovation (aside from meeting government mission requirements, such as national defense) have been met with opposition from different quarters.

Among the arguments put forth by supporters of later-stage federal investments (e.g., applied research, development efforts, and demonstration projects):

- In some cases, advocates assert, important benefits—for example, economic, social, national security—may be achieved that would not otherwise be achieved due to factors such as the absence of market incentives (e.g., development of drugs for diseases or conditions that only affect a small number of people) or the inability of a single company or group of companies to undertake such efforts due to high cost, high risk, and/or a long time horizon for achieving a return on investment. Benefits that cannot be captured by a company (or group of companies working together) that brings a product or service to market are referred to by economists as "positive externalities." Unable to capture these benefits, a company is not likely to consider them in its decision-making regarding whether to pursue the development of such a technology or product.

---

[40] See footnote 37 for information on mandatory funding and how it differs from discretionary funding.

Accordingly, economists assert that the result may be private sector underinvestment in beneficial R&D. Some analysts argue that, in such cases, public investment may be justified to induce the development of these technologies (and the realization of these benefits) by sharing costs and risks.

- Some proponents contend that such efforts are needed to ensure U.S. leadership in technologies and industries critical to U.S. national security and economic security.

- Some concerned about the competitiveness of U.S. industry posit that such efforts are needed to offset the industrial policies of other nations that make the business environment in the United States comparatively less attractive.

Among the arguments put forward by opponents of such efforts:

- According to some, such efforts constitute an *industrial policy*, resulting in distortions in markets and flows of capital by substituting governmental preferences for market forces.

- Some opponents argue that government is not able to make better decisions than markets, therefore federal funding for such activities is generally inefficient or wasted.

- Such efforts may, according to some, constitute a form of *corporate welfare*, providing direct or indirect public subsidies to for-profit corporations, enriching shareholders and others at the expense of taxpayers.

- Some opponents may assert that government funding and tax, regulatory, or policy decisions may be used to reward political supporters or punish opponents, referred to by some as *crony capitalism*.

- Others may assert that the ability to provide direct federal funding to companies or industries can lead to governmental corruption, fraud, and graft.

- Some oppose efforts such as the NNMI by asserting an absence of express authority in the Constitution to engage in such activities makes such efforts unconstitutional.

- Those concerned about the nation's fiscal condition argue that the current economic condition of the United States with respect to the budget deficit, national debt, and future financial liabilities does not allow for such expenditures, irrespective of merit and efficacy.

- **How can the NNMI contribute to the retention of manufacturing-related activities in the United States, both broadly as well as with respect to the R&D that the IMIs advance toward commercialization?**

  The innovation process can be extremely challenging. Even good ideas can fail due to a number of reasons (e.g., technical, cost, and risk barriers; disconnection from market needs; absence of standards; regulatory hurdles). A major thrust of U.S. science and technology policy has focused on how to move new ideas and insights from the laboratory into the marketplace.

  In the past, the strength of the U.S. economy and its position in the global economy largely meant that the success of U.S.-based companies in overcoming the obstacles to innovation and moving a process or product into the market resulted in production-related activities and jobs in the United States. Today, however, companies have increased options (and sometimes incentives) to establish production facilities outside the United States.

The NNMI *Preliminary Design* report states that foreign organizations with significant U.S. R&D investments and employment would be allowed to participate in an IMI if they committed to U.S.-based manufacturing for any technology arising from or assisted by the institute. Congress may want to explore how effective these requirements would be in ensuring that NNMI technology and innovations are manufactured in the United States and contribute to U.S. manufacturing employment by both U.S. companies and non-domestic organizations.

- **Which agency/agencies should lead and manage the NNMI?**

President Obama has proposed that funding for the NNMI be given to the National Institute of Standards and Technology, an agency of the U.S. Department of Commerce, through one-time mandatory funding of $1 billion to be spent over nine years. The NNMI would be managed collaboratively by NIST, DOD, DOE, NSF, and other agencies.

As the recipient of the funds, NIST appears to be the de facto lead on the initiative. In addition, the Under Secretary for Standards and Technology and Director of NIST was the only Administration official to testify at a House hearing on the NNMI in the 112th Congress.

NIST has played an important role in the federal government's efforts to support U.S. manufacturing since its establishment as the National Bureau of Standards in 1901. Beyond its core mission in measurement science (i.e., metrology) and standards, NIST took on its current name and was given additional authorities and programs by Congress in the late 1980s. Among these new programs were several programs focused on supporting U.S. firms, including the Advanced Technology Program (ATP, a program to accelerate the development of generic, pre-competitive, high-risk, high-payoff technologies; ATP was eliminated in 2007 and replaced by the Technology Innovation Program (TIP), which was subsequently eliminated);[41] the Malcolm Baldrige National Quality Award (a program to encourage the adoption of quality management principles by private companies and non-profit organizations); and the Manufacturing Extension Partnership (a program to enhance productivity and technological performance, and to strengthen the global competitiveness of small and medium-sized U.S.-based manufacturing firms).[42]

The Department of Defense is also playing a key role in the NNMI. In particular, DOD awarded the National Additive Manufacturing Innovation Institute which was described in the solicitation as "the first institute to be launched within the National Network for Manufacturing Innovation" and "a proof-of-concept for the potential subsequent institutes."[43]

---

[41] For additional information see CRS Report 95-36, *The Advanced Technology Program*, by Wendy H. Schacht.

[42] For additional information, see CRS Report 97-104, *Manufacturing Extension Partnership Program: An Overview*, by Wendy H. Schacht.

[43] *A Pilot Institute for the National Network for Manufacturing Innovation (NNMI)*, Solicitation Number BAA-12-17-PKM, Department of the Air Force, Air Force Materiel Command, May 8, 2012, https://www.fbo.gov/?s=opportunity& mode=form&id=2bbada5cae4ab97438dc3f57fed050d0.

Congress may wish to consider whether to designate a lead agency for the NNMI and to provide that agency with governance authorities and responsibilities, or whether to parse NNMI authorities and responsibilities among several agencies. Alternatively, Congress might opt to provide the Administration with flexibility to assign agency roles and responsibilities.

- **What requirements must be met for an IMI to be considered self-sustaining? With respect to federal policy, what would be the consequences for an IMI that does not become self-sustaining?**

As articulated by the Obama Administration, an IMI is to become self-sustaining no later than seven years from its award date. However, no definition of self-sustaining has been put forward by the Administration, nor is there any indication of consequences for failure to become self-sustaining. In addition, the Administration has stated that it expects that IMIs would be eligible to compete for funds for project specific activities under other (i.e., non-NNMI) federal programs.[44] How would such funding be considered with respect to the requirement for self-sustainability?

Federal requirements that organizations become self-sufficient have not always met with success. For example, the Omnibus Trade and Competitiveness Act of 1988 (P.L. 100-418), which established the NIST Manufacturing Extension Partnership program,[45] required centers to become self-sufficient within six years:

> In no event shall funding for a Center be provided by the Department of Commerce after the sixth year of the operation of a Center.[46]

Congress later amended the Manufacturing Extension Partnership program authorities in the Technology Administration Act of 1998 (P.L. 105-309) to allow centers to continue receiving federal funds if the center "has received a positive evaluation through an independent review," though it restricted funding after the sixth year to be no more than "one third of the capital and annual operating and maintenance costs of the Center."[47]

Congress may wish to consider whether to legislatively require that IMIs become self-sufficient, the time period within which self-sufficiency would need to be achieved, and the consequences of failing to do so.

- **What will be the role of the federal government, if any, in the NNMI after the end of the nine-year funding period?**

As proposed, the NNMI would receive a one-time appropriation to be spent over nine years. The Administration has not articulated its vision for the NNMI past the end of this period. Congress may wish to consider what role, if any, the federal government would play in coordinating or sustaining the network after the end of this period.

---

[44] Testimony of Patrick D. Gallagher, Under Secretary for Standards and Technology, U.S. Department of Commerce, before the U.S. Congress. See footnote 3.

[45] P.L. 100-418 uses the term "Regional Centers for the Transfer of Manufacturing Technology" to describe what is now called the Manufacturing Extension Partnership program.

[46] P.L. 100-418.

[47] P.L. 105-309. For further discussion, see CRS Report 97-104, *Manufacturing Extension Partnership Program: An Overview*, by Wendy H. Schacht.

- **What role, if any, should the federal government play in advancing technologies that can contribute to manufacturing competitiveness?**

Rapid technological advances may bring revolutionary changes to the manufacturing sector in the United States and abroad. Currently, technologies such as grid computing, multi-core processors, massively parallel supercomputers, and new modeling software allow for more expansive, less expensive, and faster testing of designs. For example, automobile manufacturers are using these technologies to supplement physical crash testing of vehicles, thereby reducing costs, increasing passenger safety, and allowing for design considerations that might not otherwise have been possible.[48] According to Ford Motor Company:

> Prior to the first XJ prototype crashing into a barrier, Jaguar engineers performed more than 500 computer-simulated crash events using sophisticated crash-modeling software and this was followed up by physical tests.[49]

Further, new technologies, materials, processes, and design tools may allow for low-cost, high-customization, small lot-size production. In addition, new collaborative innovation models may open the possibility of making once-proprietary product design processes available to external creators.

These new technologies and processes—and others that are likely to emerge from global research and development efforts—may displace existing industries, companies, and workers; change where value is created in the innovation process; and affect the competitive position of nations in manufacturing. In deciding whether to authorize and fund the NNMI, Congress may also wish to consider what the appropriate role of the federal government should be, if any, in advancing the U.S. position in manufacturing broadly (i.e., what boundaries should be set, if any, to define the appropriate roles of government and the private sector).

Author Contact Information

John F. Sargent Jr.
Specialist in Science and Technology Policy
jsargent@crs.loc.gov, 7-9147

---

[48] Deborah Wince-Smith, "High Performance Computing for All," *Issues in Science and Technology*, Summer 2009.

[49] Ford Motor Company website, http://media.ford.com/article_download.cfm?article_id=14028.